ESSENTIAL BUSINESS SKILLS

Skills required for a successful business

By: **Axel Phillips**

Table of contents

The skill of self discipline

The skill of leadership

The skill of communication

The skill of financial management

The skill of problem solving

The skill of self discipline

What exactly is self discipline? Self-discipline is the capacity to move forward, maintain motivation, and act despite any physical or mental discomfort. You demonstrate it when you consciously decide to work toward improving yourself, even in the face of obstacles like diversions, difficulty, or bad circumstances.

Self-control is distinct from willpower or self-motivation. Persistence, the capacity to carry out your ideas, and hard effort are all factors that go into it, as well as motivation and willpower.

Why should you work on your confidence?

Self-control is beneficial in many aspects of our lives.

For example, it motivates you to produce excellent work even when you don't feel like it. Even when you're ready to give up, it provides you the courage to maintain your professionalism with your clientele. It aids in your perseverance and achievement of the objectives you set for yourself. You can achieve great success through self-discipline even when the odds seem overwhelming to others.

Additionally, it can promote performance and learning. According to studies, students who exhibit a high level of self-discipline retain more information than those who do not.

Additionally, researchers found that disciplined pupils do better because they are more meticulous in their work.

The significance of self control
A successful entrepreneur needs to have some level of self-discipline regardless of the field in which they operate. It enables you to better manage your time, direct all of your efforts toward your objective, and much more.
Here's why developing self-discipline is so important if you want to succeed as an entrepreneur.

1. Increases inner fortitude
It's crucial to have inner strength when starting a business because you'll need to make sound decisions. And it

takes a lot of inner strength to accomplish this.

As an entrepreneur, you'll probably experience many ups and downs as well as difficult circumstances. You'll need to make some tough choices in response to these circumstances, as well as show your tenacity.

2. Improved Time Management
Self-discipline also involves making plans and following through on them. And if you're an entrepreneur, this element might be incredibly helpful since you'll need to manage your time very effectively.

You must utilize your time wisely because there are only 24 hours in a day. And because of this, time management is crucial.

You can arrange your day and carry it out flawlessly if you have self-discipline. It enables you to do all necessary activities and stay on schedule for the day. For instance, you can choose how much time to spend on content curation, writing, or discovery if you're engaged in content marketing.

How to Become Self-Controlled
Similar to a muscle, self-control gets stronger the more you use it and work to build it.

But it's as crucial to avoid setting overly ambitious initial goals. Instead, make modest goals and gradually raise the amount of difficulty over time. You'll get better the more you practice.

Start by implementing these five actions to discipline yourself:

1. Select a Goal
Start by deciding on only one objective you wish to concentrate on in order to improve your self-discipline.

For instance, you might decide to start working out every evening or read a leadership book every week to improve your abilities. Even very minor goals, like focusing on a task for an hour without checking your messages or abstaining from harmful foods for a

day, can help you develop
self-discipline.

Always remember that the greatest approach to begin developing your self-discipline is to start small. You can extend the emphasis to new areas of your life as your discipline grows.

Make sure your goals are SMART — specific, measurable, achievable, relevant, and time-bound — and, if you can, break them down into smaller sub-goals.

2. Discover Your Motive
After deciding on a goal, make a list of your motivations for achieving it. Make an effort to present these arguments positively.

Therefore, use the phrase "I want to exercise so that I have the energy to play with my kids and work successfully" rather than "I want to exercise three times a week to lose weight." Or, say, "I want to perform this task so that I may meet my objectives, gain praise from my supervisor, and feel content with my day's work," rather than "I want to cross this task off my To-Do List."

You'll find it much simpler to accomplish your goals if you make a list of your motivations.

3. Identify Challenges
Identify the challenges you'll probably encounter as you work toward your objective, and then come up with a plan of attack for each one.

Consider, for instance, that your objective is to improve your talents by reading one leadership book per week. You've had to overcome a lot of challenges in the past to do this. For instance, it can be challenging to find time to read every night after you find a book you enjoy. Your day is filled with work, dinner, and the kids until late at night, and while you're reading, you get interrupted by messages that come in.

4. Change Outdated Habits
When we're trying to acquire self-discipline, we frequently strive to break a negative habit and switch it out for a better one. But giving up a habit that is ingrained with a particular pattern or time of day might be difficult.

If we don't adopt a new habit in its stead, its absence will be even more apparent.

A good illustration is if you're trying to stop yourself from purchasing online during a work break. Your focus and attention are destroyed by this harmful habit because you are probably online for 20 to 30 minutes each time.

Once you've made the decision to stop, decide on a new habit you can practice whenever you need a little break. You could take a quick walk outside, get a cup of coffee, or do some stretches in your workplace instead of shopping online. Instead of leaving you with nothing to do on your break, these actions will aid in the achievement of your goal and improve your self-discipline.

5. Track Your Development
Pay attention to how you're feeling as your self-control grows and improves as you work on it. You might get a sense of liberation, joy, pride, and vigor.

Consider keeping a notebook as well to record your self-control objectives and monitor your development. This supports the constructive life adjustments you're making and provides you with a record you may review later to gauge your success.

As your self-discipline grows, you'll be able to use it in a variety of other aspects of your life.

The skill of leadership

How Do You Lead?
Leadership is a social influence technique that leverages the efforts of others in order to accomplish a goal.

Strong leaders are known to possess a number of distinct traits. The majority depend on your capacity to complete work quickly, persuade others to do well, and regularly meet and exceed expectations. There are some personality traits you already have, while there are others that you might want to work on honing. Here are a few of the traits and abilities that great corporate leaders frequently exhibit:

Self-motivation

An effective leader must be able to take initiative, which entails being able to finish work without consulting others for advice or help. You'll likely require less supervision as your competence and expertise in your job increase.

Self-motivation entails finishing a job or activity on schedule without requiring ongoing management direction or encouragement. You will rapidly distinguish yourself as a leader if you are able to do the tasks that have been assigned to you and also take the initiative to go above what has been requested of you.

Organization

Effective leaders understand how crucial it is to maintain organization at work. They keep to timetables, routinely meet deadlines, and deliver on promises. Leaders who are organized can monitor several tasks and projects at once. A team is more likely to work effectively and efficiently if the boss is a well-organized leader.

Delegation

The capacity to assign duties to other team members is a vital leadership trait. Leaders must also be able to determine when someone else might be more equipped or have more time to complete a task. A leader must be familiar with their team well enough to be aware of both their strengths and flaws in order to be able to delegate. Delegation also enables leaders to promote other capable workers into leadership positions. Leaders who delegate are better able to maximize the potential and effectiveness of their teams.

Responsibility

One of the qualities that leaders most value in their followers is responsibility. Accepting responsibility entails recognizing one's actions' effects, both good and bad. A responsible leader treats each accomplishment and setback made by their team as though it were their own. Leaders attempt to make decisions that are in the best interests of their teams and advocate on their behalf. Responsible leaders work hard to correct errors and celebrate victories while accepting every part of their role.

Setting goals Effective corporate leadership requires the capacity to concentrate on a future vision. To ensure the success and expansion of a business, executives must set strategic objectives. One of the main responsibilities of corporate leadership is to motivate all employees to collaborate in order to achieve shared objectives. One of the most crucial responsibilities of a business leader is to set realistic goals and successfully convey them to the rest of the team.

Risk-taking
Effective corporate executives are aware of the difficulties that can arise. To overcome those obstacles, they aren't hesitant to take chances and

think outside the box. Even when their choices are uncertain or unorthodox, good leaders use data to guide their judgment.

Integrity

The moral character of a team's leader is crucial to its success. It requires the leader to be honest and dedicated to doing the right thing, even when it is challenging. Integrity-driven leaders show by example. take pleasure in their job and produce successful outcomes.

Curiosity

To advance their business or team, effective leaders are always on the lookout for fresh concepts and creative solutions. The willingness to attempt new things can inspire and motivate

others to have a forward-thinking
attitude as well.

Self-awareness
You must be able to assess your own
strengths and flaws before you can do
the same for others. Good leaders are
aware of their strengths and
weaknesses and act to correct them.
By being vulnerable, team members
are motivated to stand up and possibly
take on leadership roles.

The skill of communication

Clarity depends on clear lines of communication. Being prompt in your reactions to others is an indication of good leadership and communication.

Modern technology has given us access to additional channels of communication, and the majority of us use them to communicate with various social groupings. This is both a challenge and an opportunity! You may feel overwhelmed by the constant flood of notifications. In the digital age, communication success depends on having a plan.

How will you deal with your staff? Your desk? the persons in the group? Be clear about the response times you expect. How much time should someone plan on waiting for a text, email, or phone call? Set boundaries and expectations with your team, and then hold yourself to them.

We can use a variety of modern communication methods to see if our message has been read. Facebook Messenger and WhatsApp, to name a couple, amply illustrate this. If you choose not to respond to someone after a reasonable amount of time has passed, you are not hiding. Your poor communication abilities are evident.

Communication that is swift and straightforward demonstrates integrity, respect, and leadership. As a team leader, you will cultivate their respect for this principle.

Clarity is typically hampered most by insecurity. Insecure leaders feel the need to speak in "couch" terms. What does this seem like? Whenever you catch yourself saying:

Now let's return to this if you decide to do it.
Please take your time, but if it appeals to you, maybe we could...
That's a good idea, and I'll think about it.
If you've been using it for any length of time, your staff has probably observed and abhors this terrible conduct, but they won't tell you.

By being indecisive, failing to bring conversations to a conclusion, or failing to provide a clear call to action, you irritate your team and lose their respect. By telling someone their proposal is good when it isn't or that you'll think about something when you won't, you might avoid having a difficult conversation.

Because leaders speak directly, you must learn how to do the same. The advantages of leadership are a clear direction for the team and a common goal and vision, but it also comes with tough choices.

In the church, a clearly stated objective and goal serve as a great scapegoat for suppressing undesirable thoughts. You must make sure that nothing hinders or deviates from your ministry's obvious route if you want it to succeed. Negative ideas must be dropped, no matter how well-intentioned. The challenge is to do this while respecting people, empowering them, and better integrating them into the mission and vision. Being compassionate is an effective leadership trait.

Here are some tips for improving communication to prevent miscommunications or disagreements and to promote more positive and constructive interactions:

1. THINK THROUGH YOUR SPEECH PRIOR TO SPOUTING.
Saying the incorrect thing, even at the right time, can seriously injure a

person. Imagine a situation where a doctor orders a prescription that is harmful to her patient and is inaccurate. Making a false statement in court could result in an innocent person spending a very long time behind bars. We must be careful how we communicate since words have such power. So pay close attention, give yourself some time to think before you react, and wait before you speak.

2. LISTEN QUICKLY AND SPEAK SLOWLY.

Focus on what the other person is saying and doing for a while. The majority of us hear but seldom pay attention. We frequently concentrate our resources on what we are going to say or how we will reply, rather than paying attention to and understanding what the speaker is trying to communicate. Visit Improve Your Listening Skills to learn more.

3. SPEAK UP TO HELP THE LISTENER.

Communicate with the intention of helping the recipient. Speaking is justified in many situations. There are occasions when it's only to test the relationship, as is typically the case with small talk. Some people will ponder aloud, and in such instance, your role is simply to be a listener as they attempt to process their thoughts. It might also be done to display information for whatever reason. Other times, the speaker is requesting assistance or information.

If the conversation is informal, you can help the other person by adding something to it that will be advantageous to both of you. When you're unsure about the goal of the conversation, it's polite to ask for clarification. Such a thing might be quite helpful with someone who presents something that might be a need. In circumstances like these, it's a good habit to ask, "Are you telling me this to bounce ideas off of me or because you are asking me for my help?" For more information, see this Forbes article: Here are 5 alternative questions to "How are you?" Even better, consider whether avoiding small talk could improve your mood and overall health.

No matter the situation, try to keep in mind how the speaker's listening can help the other person and the conversation.

4. SPEAK EXPLICITLY AND EXCLUSIVELY.

We frequently play games with others by not being straightforward and honest with them. This is a discipline for individuals who have mastered passive hostility. But the people we most admire are those who are true and honest. Men or women who are seen as leaders, charismatic, or who command high respect are those who can speak openly.

Being honest does not include being rude, aggressive, or using language that might be damaging. When you learn to speak the truth with grace or tact, your ability to relate with people will be liberated, and others will appreciate you for it.

5. Be aware that nonverbal communication is used frequently. Nonverbal cues lack the clarity of spoken words even if they may be more audible than those that are spoken. Nonverbal communication includes:

stance and hand motions

feelings on the face

attire & clothing

Behavior. In reality, communication forms the basis of all action.

6. LEARN THE THREE "V'S" OF SPOKEN COMMUNICATION: The spoken word is unquestionably regarded as verbal. "The majority of people concentrate simply on the verbal element expecting this to be the message although it is merely part of the full message," William Vermeulen observed in his seminars.

Resonance, projection, and intonation of the voice

Visual: your body language and expressions when conversing with people. Conscious and unconscious signals are sent by visual images. Your speaking abilities might be either improved or adversely impacted by your body language.

7. BE CAREFUL AND USE THE RIGHT WORDS AT THE RIGHT TIME.

As the saying goes, "Say what you mean, and mean what you say." It's important to realize the power of language. It's a good habit to get into to make sure you have thought through what you are going to say before you say it. The level of verbal precision depends on the urgency of the situation. A military major will surely need to talk carefully when planning an attack on the enemy, but when playing tag with your daughter, there is less need for verbal precision. But speaking the ideal thing at the incorrect time can damage the relationship or the situation.

8. WHEN NECESSARY, BE FIRM BUT TACTFUL.

Even when correcting opponents, practice using polite yet forceful words. You can appear sincere without sounding corny.

9. ACTIVELY USE QUESTIONS.

Often, the individual leading the conversation will be the one asking the questions. But sometimes the aim isn't control. By getting to the heart of the subject, insightful questions allow people to participate in the dialogue and communication process. Until there is clarification, use the "who-what-when-where-how" and occasionally "why" queries.

10. LOOK FOR MOMENTS OF IDENTIFICATION, SELF-DISCOVERY, OR TEACHABILITY.

When something significant is going to happen, pause the other person and find out their thoughts.

11. AT THIS TIME, SEEK SILENT REGISTRY.

A person seems to stop moving at this point and pauses to think about what is being said. When that occurs, it frequently indicates that your message has resonated and connected with the person or people in issue.

Nevertheless, refrain from upsetting the other individual by remaining mute. If the conversation becomes too much for you to bear at that moment, explain why you are scared to speak out and then shut it down.

12. DO EARLY RESEARCH ON THE GOAL OF A CONFERENCE.

If you are asked to meet with someone and you have any cause to assume it is not just a social or humorous request, politely suggest that they inform you in advance of the meeting's purpose.

13. CONCERNING IMPORTANT RECORDING.

This is crucial in some circumstances, including when speaking with an opponent or antagonist directly or at a meeting with a crucial committee or team. Regarding it, Winston Churchill was quite particular. I am a great believer in conducting official business through the printed word, he once said. Let it be known that I do not assume responsibility for matters regarding national defense for which I am purportedly accountable unless they are documented in writing and that any directives emanating from me must be in writing or should be confirmed in writing as soon as feasible. Stephen Hayward's Churchill on Leadership, page 110

14. CONTINUALLY COMMUNICATE PLANS AND DECISIONS TO THOSE WHO NEED TO KNOW.
15. REFUSE TO ALLOW INTERRUPTIONS.
People interrupt for a variety of reasons, but few of them contribute anything valuable or helpful to the

conversation. Some people act in this way because they are not focused. Your time and effort will be wasted if they don't listen. Because they don't respect you or the other participants in the conversation, some people interject. They are disrespecting you by acting in that way. It is challenging to conduct a conversation that benefits both parties when there is little to no respect. Respect must be shown. Some individuals interfere because they are too arrogant to believe that you have anything worthwhile to add. They need to be humble in order to interact with people in a productive and meaningful way.

Stop talking if the other person keeps interjecting, then leave.

16. Make sure unanswered questions are addressed.

Unresolved conflicts hardly ever go away on their own. Later on in your relationship, same issues frequently recur, damaging it. If you can, schedule a time to discuss any concerns that you can't resolve in your chat. Generally speaking, it is best to make that particular issue the focus of your subsequent talk.

Apply paragraphing, please.

If the topic is important enough, you should either reiterate what was stated or request that your listener(s) do the same. To determine whether the parties have a reasonable understanding, this method may be helpful. You can verify that you understood the other person's meaning by restating what they said and asking them whether that is what they meant to say or to say.

Recap meetings are 18.
After meetings, spend some time summarizing the subjects covered and the individuals who received the various responsibilities.

19. SEEK HELP IF CONVERSING WITH ANOTHER PERSON IS DIFFICULT.
Ask one or two more people to help you out if you frequently have trouble communicating with someone. This typically resolves a dispute between persons who are frequently at odds. Remember that a solution isn't always a given.

20. Give a comprehensive overview, but refrain from employing too many generalizations.
Abstract concepts should be illustrated using concrete examples. As communication experts advise, create links and describe a verbal picture.

Eradicate disturbances; 21
Put anything aside that might interfere with the quality of your speech with thought. To do this, switch off your mobile device, lock your tablet or computer, or take out your earpiece (s). Because of distractions, you are not only unable to focus entirely on the topic but also communicate to the other person that you don't find it important enough to have a meaningful conversation.

There are benefits when you put away anything that can obstruct your ability to communicate with people. Among the benefits are, but are not limited to:

being able to hold more profound discussions.

demonstrating mutual respect will almost certainly strengthen your relationship.

raising the probability that something will be finished.

You can focus more intently on each other and the agenda or topic at hand.

You can probably remember the talk's main points at a later time.

The skill of financial management

Planning, arranging, managing, and controlling financial activities, such as the acquisition and use of an organization's funds, is known as financial management. It entails applying general management ideas to the company's financial resources.

The purchase, allocation, and control of a concern's financial resources are within the purview of financial management. The goals can include

to guarantee a consistent and sufficient flow of funding to the organization.

to make sure that shareholders receive acceptable returns, which will rely on their earning potential, the share's market price, and their expectations.
to guarantee optimal use of the budget. Once funds have been secured, they should be used as efficiently and effectively as feasible. To assure safety on investment, money should be put into safe endeavors in order to get a sufficient rate of return.
To design a reliable capital structure: To maintain a balance between debt and equity capital, there should be a healthy and fair composition of capital.

Managing your finances
1. Recognize and utilize your financial reports.

The Balance Sheet, the Income
Statement, and the Statement of Cash
Flow are your three most important
financial reports. These reports
essentially outline the progress of your
company. You gain priceless
information in these reports. These
reports provide information on your
company's overall profitability, the
profit margins for each of your
products, your biggest expenses,
where you are wasting money, which
investments are successful, and a
long list of other things. Understanding
how to read these statements is in
your best advantage.

2. Establish a business operational
budget.

Consider the budget as a strategy for achieving your company's objectives. The operating budget gives you the chance to plan out your income targets, split them down by month, and figure out the costs you'll have to pay to hit those targets. It is easier to take an organized and targeted approach to attaining your business goals when you have a plan and an actionable plan.

3. Evaluate your actual progress in relation to your budget.
The best thing you can do for your business is to track your progress toward these goals as you implement your business goals. You may pinpoint where you fell short and make adjustments to your procedure the next month by keeping track of your

progress each month and seeing how close you got to achieving your goals. Monitoring enables earlier intervention to ensure you are saving time, money, and resources by enabling you to make course corrections earlier in the game, so increasing the profitability and long-term viability of your organization. Instead of failing to recognize where you are falling short, you should better position your company as you go.

4. Control your money flow
One of the main reasons why businesses fail is poor cash management. Your company's cash flow is its lifeblood, and improper cash management can have potentially negative consequences. Always make sure to pay your bills on time; if you

don't, suppliers won't want to work with you, which poses a serious risk to your company. It's crucial to control the money coming into and leaving your company.

The skill of problem solving

Implementing procedures that lessen or eliminate barriers preventing you or others from achieving operational and strategic business goals is referred to as problem-solving in the business world.

A problem in business is an instance where the intended and actual results diverge. In addition, a genuine issue frequently lacks a straightforward answer.

Business problem-solving is most effective when it is done in a systematic manner by people who:

Describe and identify the issue

Sort the issues according to their importance, size, and potential impact.
Finish the root-cause analysis.
Create a range of potential fixes.
Choose the most effective option after weighing the available options.
Create and carry out the remedy.
Why Business Problem Solving Is Important
You can grow as a leader by realizing the value of problem-solving abilities in the workplace. Your ability to solve problems will assist you in resolving important problems and conflicts that you encounter. In the workplace, problem-solving is highly regarded because it enables you to:

Utilize a common approach to problem-solving for all situations.

Locate the underlying causes of
issues.
Immediately address any brief
business interruptions
Create strategies to address long-term
issues and enhance the organization.
Consider obstacles as opportunities
During difficulties, maintain composure
How to Address Business Issues
Effectively
Although there are many diverse
problem-solving techniques, most of
them can be divided into broad steps.
Here is a four-step process for solving
business problems:

Identify the specifics of the issue.
Obtain sufficient data to precisely
define the issue. This can include
information about current operating
procedures, employee behavior,

pertinent workplace regulations, and so forth. Don't make assumptions about the appropriate course of action; instead, note the precise result that is required.

2) Creatively Brainstorm Solutions: Either by yourself or in a group, list every possible option. You'll frequently need to record them. Work with the staff who are most familiar with the problem to generate more solutions.

3) Assess Alternatives and Reach a Decision: Compare and contrast potential solutions based on their viability, taking into account both the resources required to implement them and their relative returns on investment. Decide firmly on a single solution that demonstrates how to

solve the problem's fundamental
issue.

4) Take Action: Construct a thorough
plan for executing the solution, secure
the required approvals, then execute
it.